# Not Bet
# Not W
# Just Different

## Sharon Scott
## and Nicholas, the Cocker Spaniel

**Illustrated by George Phillips**

Published by
Human Resource Development Press, Inc.
22 Amherst Road, Amherst, Massachusetts 01002
(413) 253-3488
1-800-822-2801 (U.S. and Canada)

First Printing, September, 1992

ISBN 0-87425-195-8

HUMAN RESOURCE
DEVELOPMENT PRESS

With appreciation to my mentors —

Bob Carkhuff and Bernie Berenson

# Other Books by Sharon Scott

Peer Pressure Reversal

How to Say No and Keep Your Friends

Too Smart for Trouble

Positive Peer Groups

When to Say Yes! And Make More Friends

# About the Authors

Sharon Scott is a licensed professional counselor and a licensed marriage and family therapist with over 20 years of experience. As President of Dallas-based Sharon Scott and Associates, she travels worldwide to speak to students, parents, and educators on many topics. She has trained over 1/2 million people across the United States, Canada, Malaysia, India, Micronesia, Mexico, Bermuda, and Australia in her widely acclaimed Peer Pressure Reversal skills.

Ms. Scott has her master's degree in Human Relations and Community Affairs. She formerly served for seven years as Director of the nationally recognized Dallas Police Department's First Offender Program.

She has authored five other books: *Peer Pressure Reversal, How to Say No and Keep Your Friends, Too Smart for Trouble, Positive Peer Groups*, and *When to Say Yes! And Make More Friends*.

She writes a **"Positive Parenting"** column for school district newsletters nationwide. She is a frequent local and national radio and television talk show guest, including appearances on CNN, "Good Morning Australia," and "Gary Collins' Hour Magazine." She has been quoted by numerous publications from **The Washington Post** to **Teen Magazine**.

Ms. Scott's co-author is Nicholas, her seven-year-old Cocker Spaniel. This is his second venture into writing, as he also co-authored *Too Smart for Trouble*. Nicholas has a dog obedience degree from Richland College (Class of '86). Nicholas is listed in the 1992 edition of *Who's Who of American Pets*. More importantly, he never meets a stranger! Since he was a three-month-old puppy, he has done volunteer work with Ms. Scott visiting nursing homes and doing exhibits for the humane society. When Ms. Scott is conducting workshops in the D-FW metroplex, he often accompanies her to elementary schools and is a true example of accepting everybody for "what's inside."

# Preface

When children are *very* young, they will usually make friends with anyone and everyone. This includes other children, adults of all ages, animals, and even stuffed toys! They do not discriminate because of age, sex, race, intelligence, physical difference, or brand labels worn.

Somewhere along the way, however, they learn that people are different and that society places higher value on certain physical traits. This can cause children to be unkind to one another, stare at differences, and tease unmercifully.

*Not Better... Not Worse... Just Different* has been written to help children to be kind to one another. It teaches them that it's what's inside—not outside—that really counts. In the long run, having sensitive, kind children who grow up to be sensitive, kind adults is what our world desperately needs.

There are many people whom I want to thank for helping me with this book. I appreciate my publisher's attention to detail. George Phillips has done a superb job with the delightful illustrations. I want to thank my associate, Michelle Cooper, who typed the manuscript and spent hours with me getting just the right photographs done—not an easy task when working with multiple animals and young children!

I want to thank the following young "editors" who helped me make sure the words were not too big and that the book would be interesting: Tyler Pryor, age 7; Greta Griffith, age 10; Michael Clarke, age 8; Lindsay Williams, age 9; Chelsea Williams, age 7;

John Clarke, age 6; Cameron Mason, age 8; and Rachel Griffith, age 7.

I also want to thank those students from Fairmeadows Elementary School, Duncanville, Texas, who not only read my manuscript and offered suggestions, but also served as photographic subjects for the cover and several inside pages. The students on the cover, from left to right, are:

Back Row—Joel Lopez, age 10; Angela Cardona, age 8; Tonya Cherry, age 11; Tyson Rinehart, age 10.

Middle Row—Whitney Irwin, age 5; Lindsay Irwin, age 5; Lillian Martinez, age 6; Bernard Taylor, age 7; Brian Malone, age 4; William Simnouansai, age 7.

Front Row—Craig Ivey, age 7; Nicholas, age 7; Alicia Saiyasith, age 11.

Their school counselor, H. Jane Henderson, is most appreciated for organizing the photo shoot and also offering comments on the book. Thanks also to the principal, Betsy Holschuh, who gave us all "permission slips" for this Kodak moment.

A special thank you to my animal friends, Nicholas, Shawn, Mandy, Cedric, and Katy, who really do serve as role models for kindness!

And finally, thanks to family, friends, and children everywhere, who continue to teach me so much.

Sharon Scott

July 1992
Dallas, Texas

# Table of Contents

# Chapter 1

## Meeting
## Different People

I like meeting different people!

Hi! My name is Nicholas. I am a seven-year-old Cocker Spaniel. In case you do not know, a Cocker Spaniel is a type of a dog.

Yes, I am a dog who writes books! In fact, this is the second book that I have written. My mom, Sharon Scott, helped me write the first book, called ***Too Smart for Trouble***. But I am writing this book by myself.

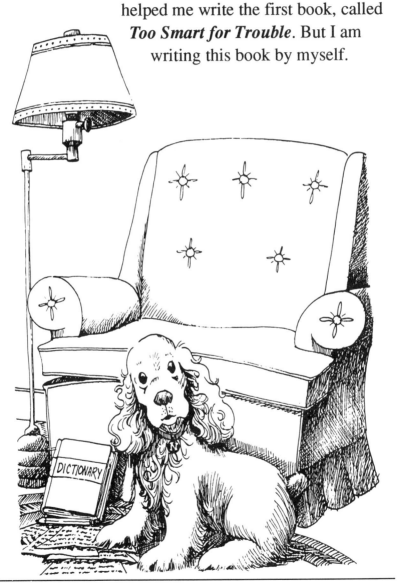

I want to tell you about some very special friends of mine. In some ways, they are all like me. In other ways, we are different. My friends' names are Shawn, Mandy, Cedric, and Katy. I will introduce you to them later.

SHAWN

CEDRIC

MANDY

KATY

Some of your friends may be a lot like you. You both may like baseball. Or maybe you both collect rocks. Perhaps you both have the same color eyes. Some of your friends are as tall as you are. Maybe some friends like to read like you do.

We often pick people as friends who like the same things we do. We may even choose friends who look a little like us. That is because we are comfortable with things that we know.

Who are some children in your school or neighborhood who are like you? How are you alike?

There are a lot of people in your school and town who are different from you. They may be older or younger. They may have a different color of skin. They may speak a different language. Some may play a sport that you have never played. Some of them may have to use a wheelchair to help them get around. Our world is filled with all kinds of people.

Who are some children in your school or neighborhood who are different from you? How are you different?

It's easy to be uncomfortable, or even scared, when we are around people who are very different from us. That is because we are not used to what is different.

My mom has traveled to many different countries. She has met people who look different, talk different, and even act different. She says it has been fun meeting these people and learning more about them.

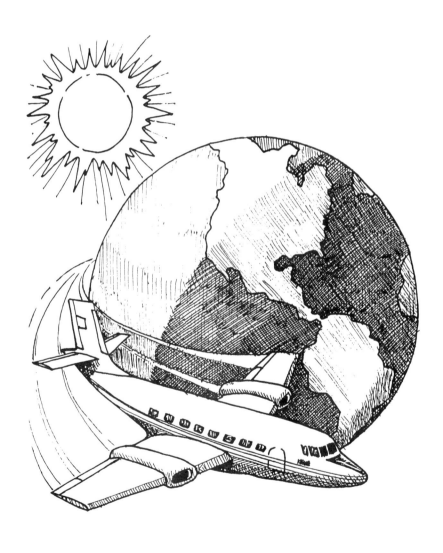

Mom said that in the country of Egypt people have brown skin. Many people live in the desert and ride camels. Some of the men wear long robes instead of pants.

When Mom went to Venice, Italy, she learned that there are no roads. There are canals filled with water. People ride in boats (called gondolas) to get around. The water canals are their roads.

She said the people in Scotland are quiet. Many of them herd sheep for a living. Some of the men wear short, plaid skirts (called kilts). They like bagpipe music.

In some parts of Africa, the people live in mud huts that they have built. Their skin is black. They live among wild animals like elephants and giraffes. The women like to make jewelry out of beads. They liked Mom's wedding ring and tried to get her to trade it for some beads. Mom could not speak their language (called Swahili). But they kind of talked to each other by acting out the words.

Mom visited a country on the other side of the world called Thailand. She learned that people live in houses built on stilts. The houses have to be built high because many people live on streams that flow from a big river (called klongs). Most of the people there are short and have skin that is yellow-brown.

Our world has a lot of different, and beautiful, people in it.

Have you ever seen a snow storm? Every snowflake is beautiful. But every snowflake is different. We are like snowflakes because we are all different from each other. And we are all beautiful in special ways.

Some of us have beautiful hair or eyes. Some of us have a great sense of humor and are funny. Some of us are beautiful because we are honest. Some of us are special because we try to be nice to everybody.

This book is about meeting people who might be different in some way from you. You will learn how to become more comfortable with each other. You will learn how to even make more friends. And, most of all, you will learn that even though we are all different, there is one way we are all the same. We all want other people to like us!

# Chapter 2
# My Friend Shawn

Shawn and I have our sweaters on this icy morning.

That is a picture of me with my friend Shawn. Shawn is my uncle. As you see, he is a Cocker Spaniel, too. I have known Shawn ever since I was a little puppy.

When I was a puppy, I sometimes acted silly. Shawn always understood that I was young, and he was nice to me. I used to even chew on Shawn's ears! He never was mean to me. He tried to teach me how I was supposed to act. He wanted me to grow up to be a nice dog.

Shawn was good at playing ball. He tried to teach me how to run fast after the ball. But he was always faster than me. We had fun playing together.

Shawn and I are alike in some ways. We both have blonde hair and long curly ears. We both have brown eyes. And we both love to go for rides in the car.

Shawn and I are also different in many ways. He is a lot older than me. Shawn is almost 13 years old. That is old in dog years. He can't run fast anymore. He walks slowly. He does not feel like playing chase anymore.

He is sometimes sick, too. He has a weak, tired heart. It can be hard for him to breathe some days. He has to go to the dog doctor a lot.

Shawn also has a handicap. A handicap is something that keeps a person (or animal) from being able to see, hear, talk, move, or think like most others. Shawn's handicap is that he is deaf. He can't hear the birds sing. He can't hear Mom call him. He can't hear me bark.

Shawn is different from me now. And I still love him so much! I even try to help him. Sometimes I walk slowly with him. I also let him know when I hear something. He watches me and can tell when someone is knocking at the door. He looks at where I am looking and knows when there is a squirrel outside the window. I have become Shawn's ears.

Do you know anyone who is deaf? Or blind and unable to see? There may be someone in your school who is unable to walk. They may have to use a wheelchair to get around. People with a handicap have to work a little harder to do some things.

Mom told me a sad story about a boy she knows. One day while Bill was riding his bicycle he was hit by a car. It was an accident. The driver did not see him when he turned a corner. Bill was badly hurt. He had many broken bones. His whole body was put in a cast. He stayed in the hospital a long, long time.

After a lot of hard work, Bill was finally able to walk again. He walked with a limp, though, because one leg was not strong yet and dragged the ground. He was so happy that he could finally go back to school. He had missed his friends and teacher.

When Bill went back to school, his classmates noticed that he walked with a limp. Many of his friends tried to help him. They carried his books and his lunch tray.

There were a few of his classmates who did not help Bill. They teased him about the way he walked and called him mean names.

Why were they unkind? Probably because they were uncomfortable about the way he walked differently. Maybe they did not know what to say. They might have been trying to show off. But they were wrong to be unkind. If they had been hurt in an accident and walked differently, they would not have wanted others to tease them.

How do you think people with a handicap want others to act around them?

Do they want people to stare at them? No!

Do they want others to laugh at their differences? No!

Do they want people to be scared to talk to them? No!

They all just want to be liked! They want to play and have friends. They want people to share toys with them. They want to be a part of games. They want people to talk to them. They want to be included.

Shawn does not want people to feel sorry for him. People who have a handicap do not want others to feel sorry for them either.

**Remember: all of us want to be liked.**

# Chapter 3
# My Friend Mandy

Sharing my toys with Mandy

That is a picture of me with my friend Mandy. Mandy is nine years old. Mom found her lost and hungry one cold, rainy day many years ago. She is a very sweet dog.

When Mom found her, she could tell that Mandy was scared. She acted as if someone had been mean to her. She would hide a lot from new people. Sometimes she would bark, too. Poor Mandy.

We do not know why someone had been mean to her. Some people act unkindly to people who have a different skin color. Mandy is a different color. She has black and white spots. Maybe someone was mean to her because she is a different color.

Our skin is different colors because of where our families came from a long, long time ago. Some people have brown skin, and some have black skin. Other people have white skin or yellow skin or red skin.

Are some skin colors better than others? Of course not.

Inside, we all have feelings of wanting to be liked. We want to have friends. We want people to talk to us. We want others to be nice to us. None of us wants to be teased or called names because our skin color is different.

The best way to get other people to be kind to us is to be kind to them. Being kind means to talk, be friendly, and act nice.

Mom says people are like a rainbow. We have different colors of skin, hair, and eyes. This makes each of us different and very special. If we all looked exactly alike, it would be boring! And we would not be able to tell who anyone was!

Mandy is happy that she has so many nice friends who do not care what color she is. Mandy just wants to be liked. She is a happy dog now.

Mandy is different from me in another way. She is a girl dog and I am a boy dog. Some people think boys are better than girls. Some people tease that girls are better than boys.

Who is better? Neither! Some girls can outrun boys. Mandy can outrun me. She is fast! Some boys can cook better than girls. It really does not matter who is best. Everyone needs to be the best they can be in everything they try to do.

*Be yourself.*

Mom says that when she was a little girl, she thought girls were supposed to have jobs like nurses or secretaries. She really wanted to be a pet doctor (called a veterinarian). But she did not think that girls could be doctors, so she did not try to become a pet doctor.

She now knows that girls can have any job they can do well. They can be doctors or plumbers or lawyers or police officers. And boys can be anything they can do well. Boys can be nurses or teachers or cooks or firemen.

You can be anything that you want to be!

Yes, Mandy and I are very different. We are good friends though. There is one big way we are alike. We both want to be liked. Just like you want to be liked, other people want to be liked, too!

# Chapter 4
# My Friend Cedric

Cedric is telling me he wants to play chase!

That is a picture of me with my friend Cedric. Cedric is an orange cat. He was born on the Fourth of July, four years ago. He did not have a home, and he lived in a little cage at the animal shelter. So my dad adopted him and brought him home to live with us.

Boy, was that a wild week! I had never seen a cat before. He was really different! Sometimes he would just sit and stare out the window for hours. And if he saw a bird, he became really excited. Sometimes he would jump in the air like he was catching something. But there was nothing there. Weird!

At first I did not like Cedric. He was too different. In fact, I even growled at him and tried to chase him away.

Mom stopped me and said, "We need to talk." She said that a cat's mind thinks differently, so he acts differently.

She said that cats were not better than dogs. I knew that! But then she said dogs were not better than cats. **Not better... not worse... just different.**

I guess I was uncomfortable around Cedric because he was different from me. I did not know what to do around him at first.

But now I know what to do. Cedric just wants to be liked. And I like him!

Cedric and I have lots of fun now. He started a game that begins when he walks up to me very slowly. Then he lightly taps me on the face with his paw. That means he wants to play chase.

He plays chase differently from a dog, though. He will suddenly stop and jump up over my back and run the other way. The first time he did that I thought he had disappeared. It was so funny!

Sometimes Cedric sneaks up when I'm asleep and bites me on the tail. He does not bite hard. He just wants to play.

Cedric thinks differently so he acts in a different way.

Some children you know may think differently, like Cedric. They may play games differently. They may do things slower. Sometimes they may give wrong answers. Remember, they may be doing their best. So it is important not to be mean to them or tease them.

Some children can't sit still for very long. They always want to move around. And some children talk when others are talking. They don't mean to be rude. They find it hard to pay attention.

And some boys and girls may do different things to get attention. They may make funny noises or faces. They may act silly. They might even shove people. They are not trying to start a fight. They may be trying to make friends, but they don't know how.

Remember, if our minds think differently, then we act differently. We should try hard to be patient with them.

I am ashamed that I growled at Cedric when I first met him. But now I know better.

I do not laugh at people's mistakes. I do not make fun when they do things differently from me.

I try to remember that we all want to be liked. And I treat others the way I want to be treated.

# Chapter 5
# My Friend Katy

I'm a hot dog and Katy is a cool cat!

That is a picture of me with my new friend, Katy. Katy is only nine weeks old. She is orange, black, and white. Mom says that a kitten with those colors is called a calico. It was a big surprise when Mom brought her home a few weeks ago.

I was really happy with just my friends Shawn, Mandy, and Cedric. And then Mom came home and told Dad that there was a cute kitten at the animal shelter who needed a home. I tried to tell them that I did not want a little sister. I thought she would be a brat and bother me. But they did not listen to me, and the next day, Mom brought home this little one-pound kitten.

They played with her a lot. They spent a lot of time wondering about what to name her and decided on Katy. Mom held her, and the kitten would actually fall asleep in her arms. I was so jealous! I was even afraid that Mom loved the kitten more than she loved me.

I got in Mom's lap and gave her a nose kiss. She
knew that I was worried that she loved Katy more than
she loved me. Mom said that she loved each of us so
very, very much. She said each one of us—Shawn,
Mandy, Cedric, Katy, and me—is so special, and she
loves us all. She said that moms and dads, grandmothers
and grandfathers, and aunts and uncles have so much
love to give that they can all love more than one child.

So now I've accepted Katy. She is really cute. She acts like a baby in the way she plays, but she *is* a baby. And now that I've started treating her nice, she has quit hissing at me!

If you have a little brother or sister, they may sometimes act silly like Katy. When you have a friend over to play, they may want to hang around, too. It's nice if you let them play for awhile with you and your friend. You might ask your parent for some special time alone with your friend, too.

Some children are so jealous of their brothers and sisters that they call them names and fight a lot. Remember that parents have so much love to give and think you *all* are great. Try to find something that you and your brother or sister like to do together, and try to become friends.

Younger children look up to you. They think you are neat. So it's good to be nice to them. You can teach them new games and how to be kind.

You, also, are younger than some kids whom you know at school or in your neighborhood. I know you want them to accept you and be nice to you. It's what's inside that counts, and that is how we should select friends. We can have friends of *many* different ages!

# Chapter 6

# Have a
# Happy Heart

Playing outside with my friend, Brian

Shawn has a handicap. And that does not have anything to do with our friendship. We are best buddies!

Mandy is a different color from me. And I think she is beautiful. Mandy and I are great friends.

Cedric acts differently from me. And I understand. Cedric and I have fun together.

And Katy is young and has a lot to learn. And I can be patient and try to teach her what she needs to know.

I try to have a happy heart. That means I like others. I try not to find fault. It also means that I love others, not hate them. It means that I do not call people bad names. It means that I do not laugh when someone tells a cruel joke.

People with happy hearts act kind. And they feel good about themselves.

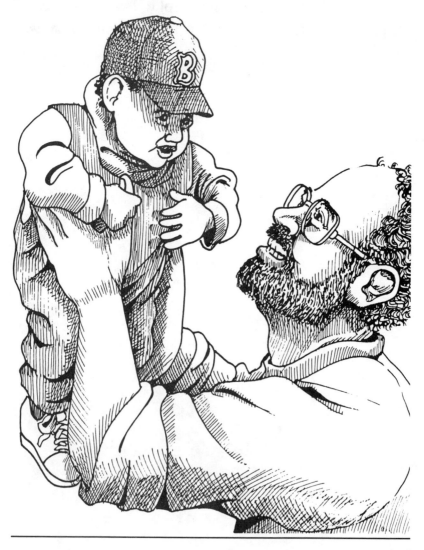

Look at the children on the front cover of this book. They are different in many ways. Some are boys and some are girls. They have many different skin colors. Several have moved to the United States from other countries and are learning to speak English. Some of these children have serious health problems. Two children have to use wheelchairs to get around. They all learn at different speeds—some very fast and others not so fast. Some of them are tall and some are short.

When I first met them, I did not notice any of those things. I noticed how nice they were to each other and to me. They all made me feel welcome at their school. They got me a drink of water. They petted me and said kind words to me. I look for what's inside because that is what's important. I like people who have happy hearts. All the boys and girls in that picture have happy hearts.

When you dislike others, you make them unhappy. It also makes you sad because you know you are not supposed to be mean. Being unkind to others does not do anybody any good!

So... how are you supposed to treat other people?

Just like you want to be treated! Be nice and kind. Everyone wants to be liked!

Here are some good ways to show kindness to everybody:

1. Look at people when you talk to them. This makes them feel important.

2. Find nice things to say about people. It's good to give compliments. If they are wearing a nice shirt or pretty dress, tell them. If they are good at playing a game or sport, let them know it. If they are funny or nice or smart, they will like it when you tell them.

3. When others make a mistake or give a wrong answer, don't laugh. That makes them feel bad. And it makes you look mean. We all sometimes give a wrong answer. Big deal!

When you talk to someone who is different from you, just treat them the same way you would want to be treated.

If someone has a different skin color from you, they are still the same inside. They want to have friends, play games, make good grades, go to recess, and do all the things that you like to do. Ask them to join in when you are playing games.

Maybe even ask them where their relatives came from. It can be fun learning about different parts of the world! Mom's family came from Scotland and Ireland a long time ago. And Mom has friends who came from Canada, Mexico, Poland, Japan, Africa, and many other places around our big world.

My family came from England a long time ago. Do you know where your family came from?

Many people have handicaps. *disabilities or impairments* Some people were born with their handicap. *disability* They may be unable to walk or talk like most of us. Some people were in an accident which caused their handicap. *disability*

People with handicaps *disabilities* have worked hard to be the best they can be. Sometimes they even have to learn to talk or walk all over again. They have a lot of courage.

It is okay to ask people about their handicap. *disability* Some may want to talk about it, and others may not. They will tell you.

Remember that all people, no matter how they look or move, have feelings. We all want to have good feelings inside.

When you see a person with a handicap, do not stare at them. They are like all of us, except they may have to use crutches or a wheelchair to get around. Some people with a handicap may have a Seeing Eye™ dog, or they may speak with their hands, using sign language. Some people with a handicap may speak slowly or take longer to say what they are thinking.

Mom is really patient with Shawn now. Since he can't hear, she taps him on the shoulder to get his attention. He knows which hand signal means to come or to lie down. He is old, and it takes him longer to eat. Sometimes she even has to help him eat. He is happy, because we treat him nice like we always have.

Here are some ideas on how to act with a person who has a handicap. *disability*

1. Look people in the eye when you talk to them. Show that you are interested in them.

2. If a person is blind, tell them who you are when you begin to talk to them. If a person is deaf, *hearing-impaired* you need to get their attention before you start talking. Maybe tap them on the shoulder.

3. If someone needs help with their books or lunch, offer to help. They will tell you how to help them.

4. Be patient. Wait for the person to finish talking. It's not nice to interrupt or correct others.

5. Ask them to join you in games, studying, and other activities. Help them to feel a part of the group. Find out what they are good at doing.

Play, talk, and have fun with lots of people. Some will be a lot like you, and some may be different from you. Other kids will think you are so special because you are nice to *everyone*.

# Chapter 7

# Treat Others the Way That You Want To Be Treated

Giving nose kisses to my friends

If you want lots of friends, then you must act like a friend. Write down how you want a good friend to act:

1. _____

2. _____

3. _____

4. _____

5. _____

I bet you wrote down things like real friends are nice, listen to you, and care about you. True friends are honest and kind to you. Good friends like to laugh and play. At times friends may argue, but they always talk it out and apologize. You can be yourself around real friends. You don't have to act cool to get them to like you. You don't have to wear certain brands of clothes to keep them your friend. Real friends like you the way you are.

It can be hard to make more new friends. Sometimes you don't know what to say. You are afraid you will say something dumb. You may think they will not like you.

I think it is easy to meet people! I just run up to them, wag my tail, and kiss them on the nose. You can too! I am just kidding you! You will meet new people in a little different way from that.

Here are some ideas to help you meet more people and make new friends.

1. Pick out someone you want to meet. Maybe they are new at your scout meeting. Maybe it is someone who just moved in to your neighborhood. Or it might be someone in your class whom you do not know. Find a time when you can walk up to them.

2. Say, "Hi! My name is _____."

3. Ask them some questions. You might ask:

   "What grade are you in?" or

   "Where do you live?" or

   "What are your favorite games?" or

   "Do you have any pets?"

4. Be good at listening when they answer your questions.

   Who is a person you do not know whom you are going to try to meet?

_____

After you meet someone new, tell them it was fun talking to them. If you want, plan something fun to do together. You might ask them over to watch a favorite TV show or to play a favorite game. Or maybe you plan to swing together at recess.

What if a new friend (or even an old friend) starts to tease other people or be unkind? Do not join in the put-downs. That might stop them when they see you do not like it.

If they keep on being unkind to others or telling mean jokes about skin color or a handicap, you may have to tell them you wish they would stop. Explain why it is unkind to put other people down. But if they keep on being mean, you really need to pick a different friend.

And if someone teases you in a mean way about your skin color or your looks or anything else, it is best just to walk away from them. Pretend you did not even hear them. Totally ignore them. It may take as many as 15 days of ignoring them, but they will stop.

If they keep on being unkind, then tell an adult whom you trust about what they are doing. The adult will try to help you.

People who tease in a mean way are trying to show off to others. If you cry or get mad, it will make them happy, and they will laugh at you. So ignore them, walk *quickly* away, and go talk to someone else or do something else.

They are probably acting mean because they are unhappy. Maybe someone has been mean to them. They probably have very little confidence. They do not know how to get attention in good ways. So they try to get attention by acting tough and being mean to others.

I surely wish everyone was nice all the time. But they are not. And it's best to get away from them when they are in a bad mood.

Do not let anyone cause you to think less of yourself. Each one of us is special. We are one of a kind—like those snowflakes!

Mom says she is a terrible swimmer. But she does not think about what she can't do well. She says she looks at the things she can do well, like snow skiing and photography.

I'm good at playing, eating my favorite snack, which is oranges, and writing books! What are you good at doing?

Think about what you can do well—your abilities. Be proud of who you are. Think positive!

And think about the kind of friend whom you like. Try to be that kind of person to others!

# Chapter 8

# What Have We Learned?

Thinking over what we have learned.

Let's add up what we have learned:

1. Treat others the way that you want to be treated.

2. Respect how each of us is different.

3. Find the good things about yourself and other people.

4. Do not judge others by what they wear or their skin color or how they walk. Judge people by how they act to you and others. It's what is inside that counts!

5. Everyone has feelings. We all want to be liked! Be kind.

Let's practice what we have learned! Read the following true stories and decide how you would handle each one.

# John's Story

John had a very long last name. It was Przywara. He was very proud that a long time ago his family had come from the country of Poland. Not many of his classmates could pronounce his name correctly. And no one could spell it except John and his parents.

When he started first grade, some of the kids at school started teasing him about his name. They called him "alphabet." They would also say his name wrong, making it sound ugly.

This hurt John a lot because he was proud of his family's name. Before you read the next page, answer how you would handle this situation if you were John.

# John's Action

At first John was so mad that he got into a fight with the kids who were calling him names. But that only got him into trouble also. He talked to his parents about it since he did not know what to do.

His dad said, "John, we are proud of our name. No one can take that away from us. Ignore them."

And John's mother added, "All these kids are trying to do is show off. They don't know how to act. If you let them know it bothers you, they will keep doing it."

The next day at school when one of the kids called him "alphabet," John just waved and went over to the swing set. He ignored them. It took more than a week for them to figure out that it no longer bothered John. But when they did, they gave up!

*Sometimes we just have to ignore other people when they are teasing to try to show off.* They will soon stop the teasing.

# Ahn Li's Story

At Ahn Li's school, a lot of kids think that to be cool you have to wear certain brands of clothes and shoes. Ahn Li did not have many of the popular brands. Her father had been laid off his job. Her family was doing the best they could with very little money.

Some of the girls at Ahn Li's school would put her down for not wearing the same brands they were wearing. Ahn Li was very sad. It was not fun to be teased like this.

Before you read the next page, answer how you would handle this situation if you were Ahn Li.

# Ahn Li's Action

Ahn Li decided that crying herself to sleep at night was not going to help. So she decided to ask some adults for help.

First, she talked to her parents. Her parents said, "Ahn Li, you go to school to learn, not to show off your clothes! And you do such a fine job learning. Your grades are good, and we are so proud of how you study every night. Try to ignore those girls at school. They don't know what is really important."

Then Ahn Li talked to her teacher. Her teacher said that she would talk to the girls and ask them to quit teasing.

Then Ahn Li talked to the school counselor who said, "Ahn Li, I know this makes you sad. I'm so glad you came to me to talk. Let's see how we can work this out." They talked for a long time. The counselor told Ahn Li there was a new girl starting school the next day. She asked Ahn Li if she would show her around. Ahn Li helped the new girl and at the same time made a new friend.

Ahn Li came to understand better that it is what's inside—*not* outside—that really matters. *And adults whom you trust will always try to help you.*

# Michael's Story

It was Field Day at Michael's school. Everyone was excited and was trying out for different contests. Michael planned to run in the grade three and grade four race. Michael was the smallest third-grade student in the whole school.

When he got in line for the race, the fourth-grade boys noticed him and started teasing about how tiny he was. They told him he should go try out in the first-grade race. They called him a "shrimp."

Of course, Michael did not like these boys treating him unkindly. Before you read the next page, answer what you would say or do if you were Michael.

# Michael's Action

Michael stood proud. He ignored the other boys. He knew that he was ready for the race. He knew that trying to do his best is what's really important.

All the third- and fourth-grade boys lined up. The race was on! Michael ran as fast as he could. He was running so fast that he felt like a bird flying.

When the blue ribbon for winning first place was handed to Michael, he felt good. He knew his months of practicing had paid off. He looked at the fourth-grade boys who teased him. They had nothing to say now. Michael was too nice to say anything bad to them. He just walked off with the blue ribbon pinned to his shirt. He saw his mom cheering in the crowd.

*What matters is trying, doing your best, and not cheating.*

# Tina's Story

Tina's family had come from Mexico. She was a very smart girl. She spoke two languages, English and Spanish. Tina had lovely brown skin and dark hair and eyes. She made good grades. Most of the kids liked her, except one girl named Sherry. Sherry did not really know Tina, but she decided she did not like her.

Sherry would tease Tina about being overweight. She would call her "brown, fat bug" and make noises like a pig when Tina walked by her. Sometimes other kids would laugh.

This hurt Tina's feelings. Before you read the next page, what would you do to solve this problem if you were Tina?

# Tina's Action

Tina told her teacher what was happening. The teacher told Tina she would be glad to try to help her. The teacher said that it might be a good idea if Tina talked to Sherry. So the teacher found a quiet time for the two girls to talk.

Tina said, "Sherry, I don't know why you tease me. It hurts my feelings. I haven't done anything to cause you not to like me, have I?"

Sherry said, "No."

Then Tina said, "I wished you would get to know me. It's what's inside that counts. Do you think we might be able to be friends?"

Sherry said, "I guess so. I'm sorry. I really didn't mean to hurt you."

They agreed not to call each other names and to say only nice things to each other. They began to get along better than ever before.

*Talking out problems with others can sometimes solve them.*

# Craig's Story

Craig was in the fourth grade. This true story is about Terrence, a classmate of his. Terrence had a disease called polio when he was a young child. He didn't do anything wrong to get it. It just happened. He had a hard time walking when he was little. But as he got older and stronger, he got better. He still had one leg and one hand that were weak, though.

At recess the boys liked to ride the merry-go-round. When Terrence got on, it was hard for him to hold on. Some of Craig's friends thought it was funny to make the merry-go-round turn so fast that it would make Terrence fall off. Terrence would cry because he did not know why some of the boys acted mean.

Before you read the next page, what would you do to help Terrence if you were Craig?

# Craig's Action

Craig did not like his friends being mean to Terrence. So he called them on the phone one night and talked to each of them. He told them that Terrence had a tough time when he was little. He said that Terrence had worked hard to do so well. He said that it was mean not to let Terrence have fun, too. Craig said, "Tomorrow at recess, let's make the merry-go-round go a little slower so that Terrence can ride it. We can go really fast some other time when he's not riding it."

Craig was surprised, but his friends all agreed to his plan. The next day at recess they let Terrence stay on the merry-go-round by not going so fast.

In fact, they got to really know Terrence. They found out that he was just another neat kid who wanted to play and have friends.

*Sometimes your friends will listen when you ask them not to be unkind to others.*

# Cassandra's Story

Cassandra was very, very smart. She was so smart that she always made 98 or 100 on her school work. Some of the kids in her class would tease her about being bright. They would call her "brain" and "teacher's pet."

Cassandra thought about making lower grades so that she would not be teased. But she knew that was not right.

Before you read the next page, what would you do if you were Cassandra?

# Cassandra's Action

Cassandra knew that grades were important. She surely wasn't going to lower her grades to please her friends. When her classmates saw her grades, it only made things worse. So she showed her grades only to her family who would be proud of her.

She understood that some kids were jealous of her. So she tried never to brag or look stuck-up.

She also asked her teacher if she could help a few of the kids with some of their work. She began showing them how to do some of their work. She also told them what a great job they were doing. Their grades went up, and they decided Cassandra was nice to help them.

*People like others who are helpful.*

# Carl's Story

Carl was a new student at school. He was scared the first day in his new school because he did not know anybody there. At lunch he sat with his class. No one talked to him though. At recess he shoved a few kids playing kickball. And in class he had trouble sitting still in his chair. He sometimes forgot to raise his hand. He would just yell out the answers. Carl was lonely. He did not know how to make friends.

If you were in Carl's class, would you try to become Carl's friend? Answer why before you read the next page.

# The Classmates' Actions

Many of Carl's classmates felt sorry for him. They knew he needed a friend. So at recess Tyrone went over and said, "Carl, let's play kickball. But please don't shove when we play." Carl said, "Okay." They had fun at recess.

During lunch several students sat with him and tried to get to know him. Keesha introduced herself. She said, "Carl, where did you live before here?" Carl answered. Then James asked, "Carl, what games do you like to play?" They found out that Carl was really good at soccer. He promised to teach them how to play it.

Carl still had a hard time sitting still in class. He still sometimes forgot to raise his hand. But now Carl felt good. He had some friends.

It's kind to make new people feel welcome. It's good to include people that may act differently. *It's what is inside that counts.*

If every person in the world used what you have learned in this book, there would be no fights… no gangs… no wars. Let's work together to make our beautiful world better for us all.

Woof! And nose kisses to you!

Nicholas

# Ending Note to Parent/Teacher:

Teaching transparencies for educators are available for *Not Better... Not Worse... Just Different* by contacting Sharon Scott's office.

And, if you would like information on how to bring Sharon Scott to speak at your school or in your community on such subjects as:

- Not Better... Not Worse... Just Different

- How to Say No and Keep Your Friends

- Too Smart for Trouble

- Peer Pressure Reversal: Survival Skills for the '90s

- Bring Out the Best! Build Kids' Confidence

- Kids Helping Kids: Develop a Positive Peer Group

then write or call:

Sharon Scott and Associates
2709 Woods Lane
Garland, Texas 75044-2807
214-495-3477

For information on ordering Sharon Scott's books:

- *Peer Pressure Reversal: An Adult Guide to Developing a Responsible Child*

- *How to Say No and Keep Your Friends* (for grades 5-12)

- *Too Smart for Trouble* (for grades K-4)

- *Positive Peer Groups* (for adults)

- *When to Say Yes! And Make More Friends* (for grades 5-12)

- *Not Better... Not Worse... Just Different* (for grades K-4)

contact:

Human Resource Development Press
22 Amherst Rd.
Amherst, Massachusetts  01002
413-253-3488
1-800-822-2801 (U.S. and Canada)

Discounts given on quantity orders.